What's in this book

This book belongs to

_____

城市设计师 City designer

学习内容 Contents

沟通 Communication

说说公共建筑和设施
Talk about public
buildings and facilities

生词 New words

★ 学校	school
★ 图书馆	library
★ 商店	shop
★ 超市	supermarket
★ 医院	hospital
★ 火车站	train station
★ 或者	either, or
★ 公园	park
设计	to design
邮局	post office
体育馆	gymnasium
电影院	cinema
银行	bank

我们还可以设计体育馆、医院或者火车站。
We can also design gymnasiums, hospitals or train stations.

别忘了公园或者电影院。
Don't forget parks or cinemas.

跨学科学习 Project

设计未来环保城市
Design a green city of
the future

文化 Cultures

世界各地古典的公共建筑
Classical public buildings
around the world

Get ready

1 Do you think the city you live in is well designed and has good facilities?

2 What is your favourite part of the city?

3 Is there anything that you would improve? Why?

shè jì
设计

如果你是城市设计师，你会怎样设计你的城市呢？

xué xiào
学校

tú shū guǎn
图书馆

你想设计更大的学校和图书馆吗？
更多的学生可以在那里学习。

shāng diàn
商店

yóu jú
邮局

chāo shì
超市

你想设计更多的邮局、商店和超市吗？我们的生活会更方便。

tǐ yù guǎn
体育馆

yī yuàn
医院

huò zhě
或者

huǒ chē zhàn
火车站

我们还可以设计体育馆、医院或者
火车站，让设施更全面。

gōng yuán
公园

diàn yǐng yuàn
电影院

别忘了公园或者电影院。休息时，大家都爱去那里。

yín háng
银行

你的城市有银行吗？你知道它在哪里吗？

Let's think

1 Which buildings are mentioned in the story? Put a tick or a cross.

2 Discuss other important public facilities with your friend. Paste your photos below and explain why they are important.

城市里还
要有……

Paste your photo here.

Paste your photo here.

城市里还要有游泳池，
因为我们要多运动。

New words

1 Learn the new words.

超市 SUPERMARKET

商店 SHOP

体育馆 GYMNASIUM

图书馆 LIBRARY

医院 HOSPITAL

邮局 POST OFFICE

公园 PARK

银行 BANK

学校 SCHOOL

设计

火车站 TRAIN STATION

电影院 CINEMA

或者

2 Listen to your teacher and point to the correct words above.

听听说说 Listen and say

04 **2** Look at the pictures. Listen to the story ar

我们一起去公园跑步。☐

我和弟弟在图书馆看书。☐

我们在电影院看电影。☐

① 星期六，你们想去哪里？

我想和爸爸去公园做运动。

③ 星期日呢？我们一起去体育馆看篮球比赛，好吗？

好！星期日见。

星期六上午，我要和爱莎去图书馆看书。下午，我要和妈妈去超市买东西。

浩浩，别忘了，星期日我们要去医院看阿姨。

我怎么忘了呢？

3 Look at the picture and complete the sentences. Write the letters.

a 医院　b 或者　c 超市　d 学校

1　浩浩坐校车去___。

2　因为伊森不舒服，所以他去___了。

3　爱莎在___门口，她想买巧克力___饼干。

Task

How many public facilities are there in your neighbourhood? Research and discuss with your friend.

Public facility	学校	超市	医院	公园	邮局	体育馆
Number						

我家旁边有……个公园和……我们可以去那里运动，很方便。你呢？

我家旁边有……我可以……我还想要……

Game

If you were a city designer, where would you build a bank in the city? Draw it on the map and discuss with your friend.

想一想，银行设计在哪里好呢？

我觉得银行可以在……旁边。因为那里有很多……从……到银行很方便。

Chant

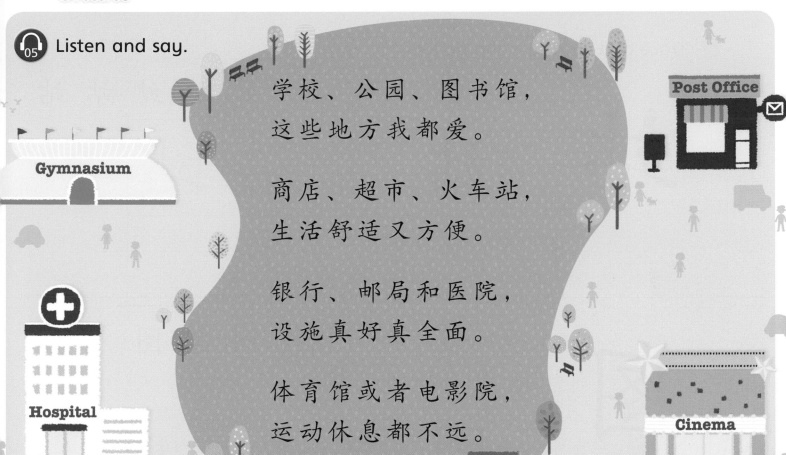

学校、公园、图书馆，
这些地方我都爱。

商店、超市、火车站，
生活舒适又方便。

银行、邮局和医院，
设施真好真全面。

体育馆或者电影院，
运动休息都不远。

Gymnasium

Hospital

Post Office

Cinema

Park

生活用语 Daily expressions

我想去······或者······
I want to go to ... or ...

15

写一写 Write

1 Trace and write the characters.

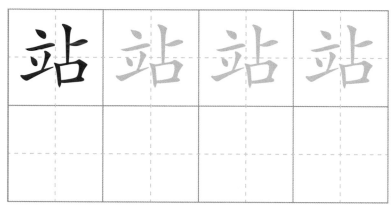

站

丶 丷 六 立 立 立 站 站 站

站	站	站	站

图

丨 冂 冂 冈 冈 冈 图 图
乛 冄 书 书

图	书	图	书

书

2 Write and say.

我想去＿＿＿＿馆看
书，你在哪里？

我在火车＿＿。

3 Fill in the blanks with the correct words. Colour the books using the same colours.

图书　从

站　中间

"请问，_____馆在哪里？"女孩问。

"在火车___旁边，你可以___公共汽车___坐车去。"我说。

"是公园和邮局_____的车___吗？"女孩问。

"不是，是医院前面的车___。"我说。

拼音输入法 Pinyin input

Write the correct letters to complete the paragraph. Compete with your friends and see who can finish typing the paragraph first.

a 很漂亮　　b 火车站旁边　　c 这是北京火车站

你知道这是哪儿吗？____。火车站的楼很高，从很远的地方也可以看见它。____有一个公园，里面有很多树和花，____！我们可以从北京火车站坐火车去很多城市，非常方便。

多元学习 Connections

Cultures

1 Learn about some classical public buildings around the world. Match the pictures to the descriptions and write the letters.

这些楼真漂亮。它们是什么呢？

这是图书馆还是邮局？你知道吗？

a Al-Qarawiyyin Library is in Morocco. It was built in the ninth century. It is one of the oldest libraries in the world.

b Kuala Lumpur Railway Station is in Malaysia. It was completed in 1910. The station is famous for its architecture.

c Hospital of the Holy Spirit is in Germany. It was built in 1332. It is one of the oldest hospitals in Europe.

2 Look at the pictures and compare the buildings. Tell your friend about the ones you like and say why.

图书馆

学校

我更喜欢上面的图书馆。因为那儿有很多树和草。

我更喜欢下面的学校。因为它的设计很……我觉得……

Project

1 Learn about environmentally friendly green cities. Match the pictures to the descriptions.

Solar panels absorb the sun's rays as a source of energy to generate electricity.

Bicycles are a form of sustainable transport. It does not use natural resources, but is cheap and efficient.

Windmills or wind turbines convert the energy in wind to generate electricity.

2 Design a green city of the future. You may use the icons. Talk about it with your friend.

绿色城市

这是我设计的绿色城市。我们用风和太阳帮助城市发电。这里有很多树和公园。这里还有……

1 Hao Hao and Ling Ling are going to visit a library. Read what they say and r⊣

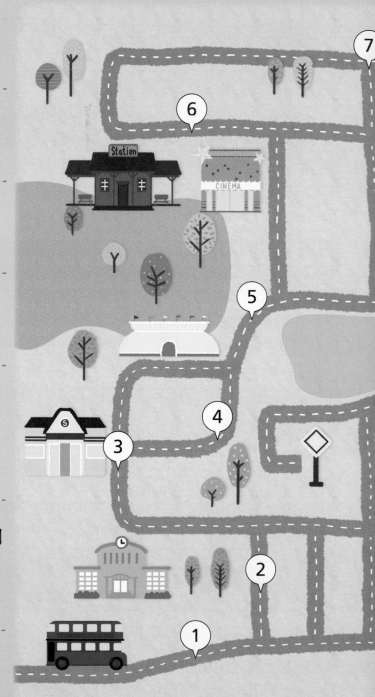

1. 从学校到邮局，坐车要多长时间？

2. 那很远。我想可能要三十分钟。

3. 你看，超市在路的左边，它真大。

4. 右边有医院，医院比超市远。

5. 我不喜欢去医院。我喜欢去公园或者体育馆，可以在那儿运动。

6. 那是火车 ☐ 吗？我们快到 ☐☐ 馆了。

7. 是的。图书馆在前面，不远了。

8. 我们快到图书馆门口了。快去看看这个有趣的地方！

2 Work with your friend. Colour the stars and the chillies.

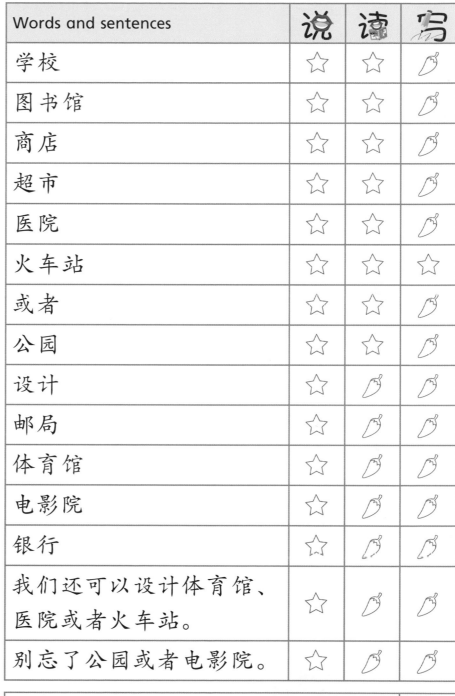

Words and sentences	说	读	写
学校	☆	☆	🌶
图书馆	☆	☆	🌶
商店	☆	☆	🌶
超市	☆	☆	🌶
医院	☆	☆	🌶
火车站	☆	☆	☆
或者	☆	☆	🌶
公园	☆	☆	🌶
设计	☆	🌶	🌶
邮局	☆	🌶	🌶
体育馆	☆	🌶	🌶
电影院	☆	🌶	🌶
银行	☆	🌶	🌶
我们还可以设计体育馆、医院或者火车站。	☆	🌶	🌶
别忘了公园或者电影院。	☆	🌶	🌶

Talk about public buildings and facilities	☆

3 What does your teacher say?

Words I remember

学校	xué xiào	school
图书馆	tú shū guǎn	library
商店	shāng diàn	shop
超市	chāo shì	supermarket
医院	yī yuàn	hospital
火车站	huǒ chē zhàn	train station
或者	huò zhě	either, or
公园	gōng yuán	park
设计	shè jì	to design
邮局	yóu jú	post office
体育馆	tǐ yù guǎn	gymnasium
电影院	diàn yǐng yuàn	cinema
银行	yín háng	bank

Other words

设计师	shè jì shī	designer
如果	rú guǒ	if
学习	xué xí	to learn
生活	shēng huó	life
让	ràng	to let
设施	shè shī	facility
全面	quán miàn	comprehensive
忘	wàng	to forget
大家	dà jiā	everybody
都	dōu	both, all
游泳池	yóu yǒng chí	swimming pool
舒适	shū shì	comfortable
发电	fā diàn	to generate electricity

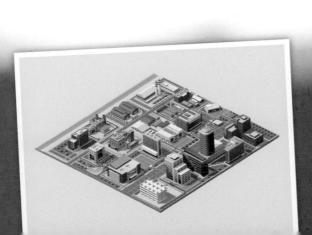

OXFORD
UNIVERSITY PRESS

Oxford University Press is a department of the University of Oxford.
It furthers the University's objective of excellence in research, scholarship,
and education by publishing worldwide. Oxford is a registered trade mark of
Oxford University Press in the UK and in certain other countries

Published in Hong Kong by
Oxford University Press (China) Limited
39th Floor, One Kowloon, 1 Wang Yuen Street, Kowloon Bay,
Hong Kong

Illustrated by Anne Lee, Emily Chan and Wildman

Photographs for reproduction permitted by Dreamstime.com

China National Publications Import & Export (Group) Corporation is an authorized distributor of
Oxford Elementary Chinese.

Please contact content@cnpiec.com.cn or 86-10-65856782

ISBN: 978-0-19-082308-5

10 9 8 7 6 5 4 3 2